WOULD YOU R...

MEET A VAMPIRE  OR A WAREWOLF

GO TO TRICK OR TREATING WITH PIRATE  OR A WITCH

WOULD YOU RATHER...

WALK THROUGH A GRAVEYARD AT MIDNIGHT **OR** **SPEND A NIGHT IN A SPOOKY ABANDONED OLD HOUSE**

DUNK FOR APPLES **OR** **CARVE A JACK-LANTERN**

WOULD YOU RATHER...

GET A SURPRISE VISIT FROM FRANKENSTEIN'S MONSTER  OR A SURPRISE VISIT FROM THE HEADLESS HORSEMAN

BE DRESSED UP AS SUPERMAN / WONDER WOMAN  OR AS BATMAN / CATWOMAN

WOULD YOU RATHER...

SPEND HALLOWEEN NIGHT AT A HAUNTED HOUSE **OR** SPEND THE NIGHT AT A CEMETERY

GO TRICK OR TREATING **OR** STAY HOME AND WATCH A SCARY MOVIE

WOULD YOU RATHER...

BE A GHOST **OR** A ZOMBIE

EAT CANDY APPLE **OR** CANDY CORN

WOULD YOU RATHER...

GO TO A REAL HAUNTED HOUSE **OR** WATCH A HORROR MOVIE MARATHON

GO TRICK OR TREATING **OR** GO OUT ON A DATE

WOULD YOU RATHER...

HAVE A CREATIVE COSTUME  OR A SCARY COSTUME

VISIT A CEMETERY  OR VISIT A PET CEMETERY AT MIDNIGHT

WOULD YOU RATHER...

WATCH A SCARY MOVIE WITH A SCARY MOVIE BUFF **OR** WATCH A SCARY MOVIE WITH A SCAREDY CAT

BE ABSOLUTELY TERRIFIED OF THE DARK **OR** BE AFRAID OF THE THE THING UNDERNEATH YOUR BED

WOULD YOU RATHER...

HAVE A HALLOWEEN PARTY **OR** A CHRISTMAS PARTY

GO TRICK OR TREATING AS A KID **OR** AS AN ADULT WITH YOUR KIDS?

WOULD YOU RATHER...

GET ATTACKED BY A GIANT SPIDER  OR A SPOOKY SKELETON

EAT CANDY EVERY DAY FOR A MONTH  OR HAVE NO CANDY FOR A MONTH

WOULD YOU RATHER...

EAT CANDY CORN  OR MARSHMALLOWS

VISIT A HAUNTED HOUSE  OR A HAUNTED GRAVEYARD

WOULD YOU RATHER...

BE SCARED  OR MAKE SOMEONE ELSE SCARED

GIVE OUT CANDY  OR TAKE CANDY

WOULD YOU RATHER...

RISK GETTING TRICKED  OR GIVE OUR KING SIZED CANDIES ALL NIGHT

TRICK OR TREAT IN YOUR NEIGHBORHOOD  OR A DIFFERENT NEIGHBORHOOD

WOULD YOU RATHER...

GO TRICK OR TREATING WITH A GROUP OF FRIENDS  **OR** WITH A GROUP OF FAMILY MEMBERS

HAVE CANDY FOR DINNER  **OR** HAVE CANDY FOR BREAKFAST

WOULD YOU RATHER...

EAT ALL YOUR HALLOWEEN CANDY IN ONE NIGHT  OR AT ONE PIECE EVERY DAY FOR A YEAR

DRESS UP AS A DEVIL  OR DRESS UP AS A ANGEL

WOULD YOU RATHER...

BE CHASED BY FIVE ZOMBIES  OR BE CHASED BY ONE WEREWOLF

HAVE TO SLEEP IN A COFIN  OR HAVE TO LIVE IN A GIANT PUMPKIN

WOULD YOU RATHER...

HAVE A HOMEMADE COSTUME  OR HAVE A STORE-BOUGHT COSTUME

READ A SPOOKY STORY  OR SEE A SPOOKIE MOVIE

WOULD YOU RATHER...

HAVE TO EAT 6 EYEBALLS  OR HAVE TO EAT A SMALL FROG

EAT A PLATE FULL OF WORMS  OR EAT A MYSTERY MEAT

WOULD YOU RATHER...

BE IN ROOM WITH 100 SPIDERS  **OR** **100 BATS**

GO TO PARTY WITH WITCHES  **OR** **WITH DEMONS**

WOULD YOU RATHER...

EAT ALL YOUR CANDY **OR** TRADE YOUR CANDY FOR 10$

BE A JOKER **OR** BE A BATMAN

WOULD YOU RATHER...

GET ONLY CHOCKOLATE CANDY  **OR** **GET ONLY GUMMY CANDY**

FACE A ZOMBIE APOCALYPSE  **OR** **AN INVASION OF 10-FT SPIDERS**

Made in the USA
Monee, IL
29 October 2020

46316035R00024